Generative AI and Deep Learning: From Fundamentals to Advanced Applications

Table of Contents

- Neural Networks Basics

- Activation Functions

- Training Neural Networks

- Optimization Techniques

3. **Deep Learning Architectures**

- Convolutional Neural Networks (CNNs)

- Recurrent Neural Networks (RNNs)

- Long Short-Term Memory (LSTM)

- Transformer Models

Part II: Generative Models

4. Overview of Generative Models

- What are Generative Models?

- Types of Generative Models

- Applications of Generative Models

5. Autoencoders

- Introduction to Autoencoders

- Variational Autoencoders (VAEs)

- Applications of Autoencoders

6. Generative Adversarial Networks (GANs)

- Introduction to GANs

- Architecture of GANs

- Training GANs

- Variants of GANs (DCGAN, StyleGAN, CycleGAN)

- Applications of GANs

7.**Other Generative Models**

- Restricted Boltzmann Machines (RBMs)

- Deep Belief Networks (DBNs)

- Normalizing Flows

- Diffusion Models

Part III: Advanced Topics in Generative AI

10. Generative AI in Computer Vision

- Image Generation

- Style Transfer

- Super-Resolution

11. Ethics and Challenges in Generative AI

- Ethical Considerations

- Bias and Fairness

- Security Concerns

- Future Challenges

Part IV: Practical Applications and Case Studies

12. Generative AI in Art and Creativity

- AI-generated Art
- Music and Literature

13. Generative AI in Healthcare

- Drug Discovery
- Medical Imaging
- Personalized Medicine

14. Generative AI in Business

- Marketing and Advertising

- Customer Service and Chatbots

- Financial Modeling

15. **Case Studies**

   - Real-world Implementations

   - Success Stories

   - Lessons Learned

Part V: Tools and Frameworks

16. **Deep Learning Frameworks**

   - TensorFlow

- PyTorch

- Keras

17. **Generative AI Tools and Libraries**

- OpenAI GPT

- StyleGAN

- DeepArt

18. **Building and Deploying Generative Models**

- Model Training and Evaluation

- Deployment Strategies

- Scaling and Optimization

Part VI: Future Directions

19. The Future of Generative AI and Deep Learning

- Emerging Trends

- Research Directions

- Impact on Society

20. Conclusion

- Recap of Key Concepts

- Final Thoughts

Part I: Introduction to Generative AI and Deep Learning

Chapter 1: Introduction

What is Generative AI? Generative AI refers to algorithms that can create new content, such as images, music, text, or even complex models. These algorithms learn patterns from input data and generate similar outputs, allowing for creative and innovative applications across various domains.

What is Deep Learning? Deep Learning is a subset of machine learning involving neural networks with many layers (deep neural networks). It is particularly effective in processing large amounts of unstructured data, such as images, audio, and text, and has revolutionized fields like computer vision, natural language processing, and speech recognition.

History and Evolution of AI and Deep Learning The journey of AI began with simple rule-based systems and has evolved through several waves of innovation. Key milestones include the development of neural networks, the backpropagation algorithm, the resurgence of interest in the 2000s, and the explosion of deep learning techniques in the 2010s, driven by advances in computational power and large datasets.

Key Applications and Impact Generative AI and deep learning have numerous applications: image and video synthesis, text generation, drug discovery, autonomous vehicles, and personalized recommendations.

These technologies are transforming industries, driving innovation, and raising important ethical and societal considerations.

Chapter 2: Fundamentals of Deep Learning

Neural Networks Basics Neural networks are computational models inspired by the human brain, consisting of interconnected nodes (neurons) organized in layers. Each neuron processes inputs, applies a weighted sum, and passes the result through an activation function to produce an output.

Activation Functions Activation functions introduce non-linearity into the network, enabling it to learn complex patterns. Common activation functions include the sigmoid, hyperbolic tangent (tanh), and rectified linear unit (ReLU).

Training Neural Networks Training a neural network involves adjusting the weights of connections based on the error (loss) between the predicted and actual outputs. This process typically uses gradient descent and backpropagation to minimize the loss function iteratively.

Optimization Techniques Optimization techniques enhance the efficiency and effectiveness of training neural networks. These include stochastic gradient descent (SGD), momentum, Adam optimizer, and learning rate schedules. Regularization methods like dropout and batch normalization help prevent overfitting and improve generalization.

Chapter 3: Deep Learning Architectures

Convolutional Neural Networks (CNNs)

CNNs are designed for processing grid-like data, such as images. They use convolutional layers to extract features through filters that scan the input, pooling layers to reduce dimensionality, and fully connected layers to make predictions. CNNs are widely used in image recognition, object detection, and other computer vision tasks.

Recurrent Neural Networks (RNNs) RNNs are specialized for sequential data, such as time series or text. They maintain a hidden state that captures information from previous steps, enabling them to model temporal dependencies. Variants like bidirectional RNNs and gated architectures enhance their performance.

Long Short-Term Memory (LSTM) LSTMs are a type of RNN designed to address the vanishing gradient problem, which hampers the learning of long-range dependencies.

They use gates (input, forget, and output) to control the flow of information, making them effective for tasks like language modeling and sequence prediction.

Transformer Models Transformers are a breakthrough in deep learning for sequential data. They rely on self-attention mechanisms to weigh the importance of different parts of the input, enabling parallel processing and capturing long-range dependencies more efficiently. Transformer models, like BERT and

GPT, have achieved state-of-the-art results in natural language processing tasks.

Part II: Generative Models

Chapter 4: Overview of Generative Models

What are Generative Models?

Generative models are a class of machine learning models that can generate new data samples from the learned distribution of the input data. Unlike discriminative models, which focus on predicting labels given input data, generative models aim to understand

and capture the underlying data distribution to create new, similar instances.

Types of Generative Models

1. **Autoencoders (AEs)**: Neural networks designed to learn efficient representations of data by encoding inputs into a lower-dimensional space and then reconstructing them.

2. **Variational Autoencoders (VAEs)**: A type of autoencoder that introduces probabilistic elements, allowing for the

generation of new data points by sampling from the learned latent space.

3. **Generative Adversarial Networks (GANs)**: Consist of two neural networks, a generator and a discriminator, that compete in a game-theoretic framework to produce realistic data samples.

4. **Restricted Boltzmann Machines (RBMs)**: A type of stochastic neural network used to learn probability distributions over a set of inputs.

5. **Normalizing Flows**: Techniques that transform a simple distribution into a complex one using a series of invertible transformations.

Applications of Generative Models

- **Image Generation**: Creating realistic images from random noise or specified conditions.

- **Text Generation**: Producing coherent and contextually relevant text, such as articles, poetry, or dialogue.

- **Data Augmentation**: Increasing the diversity of training datasets to improve model performance.

- **Drug Discovery**: Generating potential drug molecules by exploring chemical space.

- **Art and Creativity**: Assisting in the creation of artworks, music, and other creative endeavors.

Chapter 5: Autoencoders

Introduction to Autoencoders

Autoencoders are neural networks designed to learn low-dimensional representations (encodings) of data. They consist of two main parts:

- **Encoder**: Compresses the input into a latent space representation.
- **Decoder**: Reconstructs the input from the latent representation.

Autoencoders are trained to minimize the difference between the input and the reconstructed output, effectively learning the most important features of the data.

Example Code: Basic Autoencoder in Python with Keras

python

Copy code

```
import numpy as np from keras.layers import
Input, Dense from keras.models import Model
from keras.datasets import mnist # Load data
```

```python
(x_train, _), (x_test, _) = mnist.load_data()
x_train = x_train.astype('float32') / 255. x_test
= x_test.astype('float32') / 255. x_train =
x_train.reshape((len(x_train),
np.prod(x_train.shape[1:])))         x_test         =
x_test.reshape((len(x_test),
np.prod(x_test.shape[1:]))   #   Define   the
autoencoder       model       input_dim       =
x_train.shape[1] encoding_dim = 32 input_img
=    Input(shape=(input_dim,))    encoded    =
Dense(encoding_dim,
activation='relu')(input_img)       decoded      =
```

```python
Dense(input_dim,
activation='sigmoid')(encoded) autoencoder =
Model(input_img,                        decoded)
autoencoder.compile(optimizer='adam',
loss='binary_crossentropy') # Train the model
autoencoder.fit(x_train,  x_train,  epochs=50,
batch_size=256,                   shuffle=True,
validation_data=(x_test, x_test)) # Encode and
decode   some   digits   encoded_imgs   =
autoencoder.predict(x_test)
```

Variational Autoencoders (VAEs)

VAEs extend the concept of autoencoders by introducing a probabilistic approach to the latent space. Instead of mapping inputs to a fixed latent vector, VAEs map inputs to a distribution over the latent space, typically a Gaussian distribution. This allows for the generation of new data samples by sampling from the learned distribution.

Example Code: Basic VAE in Python with Keras

python

Copy code

```
import numpy as np from keras.layers import
Input, Dense, Lambda from keras.models
import Model from keras.losses import
binary_crossentropy from keras import
backend as K from keras.datasets import
mnist # Load data (x_train, _), (x_test, _) =
mnist.load_data()                x_train       =
x_train.astype('float32')  /  255.  x_test  =
x_test.astype('float32')  /  255.  x_train  =
x_train.reshape((len(x_train),
```

```
np.prod(x_train.shape[1:]))) x_test =

x_test.reshape((len(x_test),

np.prod(x_test.shape[1:]))) # Define VAE

model input_dim = x_train.shape[1] latent_dim

= 2 inputs = Input(shape=(input_dim,)) h =

Dense(256, activation='relu')(inputs) z_mean

= Dense(latent_dim)(h) z_log_var =

Dense(latent_dim)(h) def sampling(args):

z_mean, z_log_var = args epsilon =

K.random_normal(shape=(K.shape(z_mean)[0],

latent_dim), mean=0., stddev=0.1) return

z_mean + K.exp(z_log_var) * epsilon z =
```

```python
Lambda(sampling, output_shape=(latent_dim,))([z_mean, z_log_var]) decoder_h = Dense(256, activation='relu') decoder_mean = Dense(input_dim, activation='sigmoid') h_decoded = decoder_h(z) x_decoded_mean = decoder_mean(h_decoded) vae = Model(inputs, x_decoded_mean) # Loss function xent_loss = binary_crossentropy(inputs, x_decoded_mean) kl_loss = - 0.5 * K.mean(1 + z_log_var - K.square(z_mean) - K.exp(z_log_var), axis=-1) vae_loss = xent_loss + kl_loss
```

```
vae.add_loss(vae_loss)

vae.compile(optimizer='rmsprop') # Train the

VAE    vae.fit(x_train,    x_train,    epochs=50,

batch_size=256, validation_data=(x_test, None))

#  Generate  new  digits  new_samples  =

np.random.normal(size=(10,       latent_dim))

generated_digits = vae.predict(new_samples)
```

Applications of Autoencoders

- **Dimensionality Reduction**: Autoencoders can reduce the dimensionality of data, making it easier to visualize and analyze.

- **Denoising**: Denoising autoencoders can learn to remove noise from input data, improving the quality of signals or images.

- **Anomaly Detection**: Autoencoders can be trained on normal data to learn typical patterns. When presented with anomalous data, the reconstruction error will be higher, making it useful for detecting anomalies.

Use Case: Anomaly Detection with Autoencoders Imagine a manufacturing process where sensors collect data on machinery operation. By training an autoencoder on data from normal operation, it can learn the typical behavior of the machinery. If the autoencoder encounters data from a faulty operation, it will struggle to reconstruct it accurately, indicating an anomaly.

Example Scenario A factory uses an autoencoder to monitor vibrations in machinery. During normal operation, the reconstruction error is low. One day, the error spikes, alerting the maintenance team to a potential issue. They investigate and find a loose part causing abnormal vibrations, preventing a possible breakdown.

Chapter 6: Generative Adversarial Networks (GANs)

Introduction to GANs

Generative Adversarial Networks (GANs) are a type of generative model introduced by Ian Goodfellow and his colleagues in 2014. GANs consist of two neural networks, a generator and a discriminator, which are trained simultaneously through adversarial processes. The generator creates fake data samples, while the discriminator evaluates whether the samples are real or fake.

Key Components:

- **Generator (G)**: Takes random noise as input and generates data samples.

- **Discriminator (D)**: Takes both real and fake data samples as input and tries to distinguish between them.

The goal of the generator is to produce data so realistic that the discriminator cannot tell the difference, while the discriminator's goal is to correctly identify real and fake samples.

Example Code: Basic GAN in Python with Keras

python

Copy code

```
import numpy as np from keras.models import
Sequential from keras.layers import Dense,
LeakyReLU from keras.optimizers import
Adam from keras.datasets import mnist #
Load and preprocess data (x_train, _), (_, _) =
mnist.load_data()                    x_train                =
(x_train.astype('float32')  -  127.5)  /  127.5
x_train   =   x_train.reshape((x_train.shape[0],
```

```python
784)) # Define the generator model generator
= Sequential([ Dense(256, input_dim=100),
LeakyReLU(alpha=0.2),                    Dense(512),
LeakyReLU(alpha=0.2),                   Dense(1024),
LeakyReLU(alpha=0.2),                    Dense(784,
activation='tanh') ]) # Define the discriminator
model       discriminator     =      Sequential([
Dense(1024,                       input_dim=784),
LeakyReLU(alpha=0.2),                    Dense(512),
LeakyReLU(alpha=0.2),                    Dense(256),
LeakyReLU(alpha=0.2),                      Dense(1,
activation='sigmoid')                           ])
```

```
discriminator.compile(optimizer=Adam(0.000
2, 0.5), loss='binary_crossentropy') # Define
the combined model discriminator.trainable =
False      gan      =      Sequential([generator,
discriminator])
gan.compile(optimizer=Adam(0.0002,      0.5),
loss='binary_crossentropy')  #  Training  the
GAN  def  train_gan(epochs,  batch_size):  for
epoch in range(epochs): # Train discriminator
idx  =  np.random.randint(0,  x_train.shape[0],
batch_size) real_images = x_train[idx] noise =
np.random.normal(0,  1,  (batch_size,  100))
```

```python
fake_images = generator.predict(noise)
d_loss_real = discriminator.train_on_batch(real_images,
np.ones((batch_size, 1))) d_loss_fake =
discriminator.train_on_batch(fake_images,
np.zeros((batch_size, 1))) d_loss = 0.5 *
np.add(d_loss_real, d_loss_fake) # Train
generator noise = np.random.normal(0, 1,
(batch_size, 100)) valid_y = np.array([1] *
batch_size) g_loss = gan.train_on_batch(noise,
valid_y) print(f"Epoch {epoch+1}/{epochs} | D
```

Loss: {d_loss} | G Loss: {g_loss}")

```
train_gan(epochs=10000, batch_size=64)
```

Variants of GANs

1. **Deep Convolutional GANs (DCGANs)**: Use convolutional layers to improve the quality of generated images.

2. **Conditional GANs (cGANs)**: Generate data conditioned on additional information, such as class labels.

3. **StyleGANs**: Allow for control over the style and features of generated images,

producing high-quality and diverse outputs.

4. **CycleGANs**: Enable image-to-image translation without requiring paired examples.

Applications of GANs

- **Image Generation**: Creating high-resolution and realistic images for art, design, and entertainment.

- **Data Augmentation**: Generating synthetic data to augment training datasets, improving model performance.

- **Super-Resolution**: Enhancing the resolution of low-quality images, useful in medical imaging and surveillance.

- **Style Transfer**: Applying the style of one image to the content of another, used in art and creative applications.

- **Text-to-Image Synthesis**: Generating images from textual descriptions, useful in content creation and design.

Case Study: Using GANs for Super-Resolution A leading medical imaging company wanted to improve the resolution of

MRI scans. They used a GAN-based model to enhance the resolution of low-quality scans, enabling doctors to detect anomalies with greater accuracy. The GAN was trained on a dataset of high- and low-resolution scan pairs, learning to produce high-resolution images from low-resolution inputs.

Part II: Generative Models

Chapter 7: Other Generative Models

Restricted Boltzmann Machines (RBMs)

Restricted Boltzmann Machines (RBMs) are stochastic neural networks capable of learning a probability distribution over their input data. They consist of a visible layer and a hidden layer with symmetric connections between them, but no connections within a layer.

Use Case: Collaborative Filtering RBMs are commonly used for recommendation systems.

For instance, Netflix employs RBMs to analyze user preferences and recommend movies based on the learned patterns of viewing habits.

Example Code: Basic RBM in Python

python

Copy code

```
import numpy as np from sklearn.neural_network import BernoulliRBM from sklearn.datasets import fetch_openml from sklearn.preprocessing import MinMaxScaler # Load data mnist =
```

```
fetch_openml('mnist_784') X = mnist.data X =
MinMaxScaler().fit_transform(X) # Define and
train          RBM          rbm          =
BernoulliRBM(n_components=256,
learning_rate=0.01, n_iter=10, random_state=0)
rbm.fit(X) # Transform data X_transformed =
rbm.transform(X) print(X_transformed.shape)
```

Deep Belief Networks (DBNs)

Deep Belief Networks (DBNs) are a stack of
RBMs where each layer's hidden units serve as
the visible units for the next layer. They are

trained in a greedy layer-by-layer manner and are effective for unsupervised learning tasks.

Use Case: Image Recognition DBNs can be used to recognize patterns in images. For example, they can be trained on a dataset of handwritten digits to identify and classify new handwritten inputs.

Example Scenario A DBN is trained on the MNIST dataset for digit recognition. Each layer of the DBN extracts increasingly abstract features of the input images, improving the classification accuracy.

Normalizing Flows

Normalizing Flows transform a simple probability distribution (like a Gaussian) into a more complex distribution using a series of invertible transformations. They provide exact likelihood evaluation and efficient sampling.

Use Case: Density Estimation Normalizing flows are used for density estimation in scenarios where modeling the probability density function is crucial, such as in anomaly detection for network security.

Example Code: Basic Normalizing Flow in Python with TensorFlow

python

Copy code

```
import tensorflow as tf import tensorflow_probability as tfp # Define a simple bijector (e.g., affine) bijector = tfp.bijectors.Affine(scale_tril=[[1.0]]) # Define a base distribution base_distribution = tfp.distributions.MultivariateNormalDiag(loc=[
```

```
0.0]) # Create a transformed distribution
transformed_distribution =
tfp.distributions.TransformedDistribution(
distribution=base_distribution,
bijector=bijector ) # Sample from the
transformed distribution samples =
transformed_distribution.sample(1000)
print(samples.numpy())
```

Diffusion Models

Diffusion Models generate data by reversing a diffusion process, which gradually adds noise to the data. These models learn to invert this process, effectively denoising the data to generate new samples.

Use Case: Image Synthesis Diffusion models are used in high-quality image synthesis. They iteratively refine a noisy image until it becomes a clear and detailed picture, useful in creative industries for generating art and designs.

Example Scenario A diffusion model is trained to generate images of human faces. Starting from a noise pattern, the model refines the image through multiple steps until a realistic face emerges, providing high-quality results suitable for digital art.

Part III: Advanced Topics in Generative AI

Chapter 8: Reinforcement Learning and Generative Models

Basics of Reinforcement Learning

Reinforcement Learning (RL) involves an agent that learns to make decisions by performing actions in an environment to maximize cumulative reward. The agent receives feedback through rewards or penalties and uses this to

update its strategy, known as the policy, to improve performance over time.

Key Concepts:

- **Agent**: The learner or decision-maker.

- **Environment**: The external system the agent interacts with.

- **Action**: Choices the agent makes.

- **State**: The current situation of the environment.

- **Reward**: Feedback from the environment.

- **Policy**: The strategy the agent employs to choose actions.

Integrating Reinforcement Learning with Generative Models

Combining RL with generative models enhances both fields. Generative models can create realistic simulations for RL training, while RL can help improve generative models by optimizing generation strategies.

Use Case: Game Development In video game development, generative models can create complex environments or levels, while RL agents learn to navigate and succeed in these environments, providing a dynamic and engaging gaming experience.

Example Scenario A game developer uses a GAN to generate diverse levels for a platform game. An RL agent is then trained to play these levels, learning strategies to overcome various obstacles. The GAN ensures endless new levels, while the RL agent improves its gameplay skills.

Chapter 9: Generative AI in Natural Language Processing

Language Models

Language models are a type of generative model specifically designed to handle text data. They predict the probability of a sequence of words and can generate coherent and contextually relevant text.

Example Code: Simple Language Model with GPT-2 in Python

python

```
Copy code

from transformers import GPT2LMHeadModel,
GPT2Tokenizer # Load pre-trained model and
tokenizer model_name = 'gpt2' model =
GPT2LMHeadModel.from_pretrained(model_na
me)                    tokenizer              =
GPT2Tokenizer.from_pretrained(model_name)
# Encode input text input_text = "Once upon a
time" input_ids = tokenizer.encode(input_text,
return_tensors='pt') # Generate text output =
model.generate(input_ids,      max_length=50,
num_return_sequences=1)   generated_text   =
```

```
tokenizer.decode(output[0],

skip_special_tokens=True)

print(generated_text)
```

Text Generation

Text generation involves creating new textual content from learned patterns in existing data. This can include tasks like story writing, poetry, and automated reporting.

Use Case: Automated News Writing News agencies can use text generation models to draft articles based on data inputs, such as financial reports or sports events, saving time and ensuring timely publication.

Example Scenario A news agency uses a GPT model to generate financial news articles. The model is fed with the latest stock market data and generates coherent, informative articles that are reviewed by editors before publication.

Transformers and Attention Mechanisms (BERT, GPT)

Transformers are the backbone of many state-of-the-art NLP models. They use self-attention mechanisms to weigh the importance of different words in a sequence, enabling the capture of long-range dependencies and context.

Key Models:

- **BERT (Bidirectional Encoder Representations from Transformers):**

Pre-trained on a large corpus of text, BERT can be fine-tuned for various NLP tasks like question answering and sentiment analysis.

- **GPT (Generative Pre-trained Transformer)**: A model designed for text generation, trained to predict the next word in a sequence, making it powerful for generating coherent text.

Example Code: Using BERT for Sentiment Analysis

```python
from transformers import BertTokenizer, BertForSequenceClassification
from transformers import pipeline

# Load pre-trained model and tokenizer
model_name = 'bert-base-uncased'
model = BertForSequenceClassification.from_pretrained(model_name)
tokenizer = BertTokenizer.from_pretrained(model_name)

# Create a sentiment analysis pipeline
nlp = pipeline('sentiment-analysis', model=model,
```

```
tokenizer=tokenizer) # Analyze sentiment text
= "I love generative AI!" result = nlp(text)
print(result)
```

This section provides a comprehensive overview of other generative models such as RBMs, DBNs, normalizing flows, and diffusion models, including practical examples and use cases. It also introduces advanced topics in generative AI, such as the integration of reinforcement learning and the application of generative models in natural language processing, with code snippets to illustrate key concepts. The next sections will delve deeper into real-world applications, ethical considerations, and future directions in generative AI and deep learning.

Part III: Generative AI in Computer Vision

Chapter 10: Image Generation

Image generation with generative AI involves creating new, synthetic images from learned patterns in existing data. Techniques like Generative Adversarial Networks (GANs) have revolutionized this field, enabling the creation of highly realistic images.

Example Code: Basic GAN for Image Generation

python

Copy code

```
import numpy as np from keras.models import
Sequential from keras.layers import Dense,
LeakyReLU from keras.optimizers import
Adam from keras.datasets import mnist #
Load and preprocess data (x_train, _), (_, _) =
mnist.load_data()          x_train          =
(x_train.astype('float32') - 127.5) / 127.5
x_train = x_train.reshape((x_train.shape[0],
```

```python
784)) # Define the generator model generator
= Sequential([ Dense(256, input_dim=100),
LeakyReLU(alpha=0.2),                    Dense(512),
LeakyReLU(alpha=0.2),                    Dense(1024),
LeakyReLU(alpha=0.2),                    Dense(784,
activation='tanh') ]) # Define the discriminator
model    discriminator    =    Sequential([
Dense(1024,                    input_dim=784),
LeakyReLU(alpha=0.2),                    Dense(512),
LeakyReLU(alpha=0.2),                    Dense(256),
LeakyReLU(alpha=0.2),                    Dense(1,
activation='sigmoid')                    ])
```

```python
discriminator.compile(optimizer=Adam(0.0002, 0.5), loss='binary_crossentropy') # Define the combined model discriminator.trainable = False gan = Sequential([generator, discriminator])

gan.compile(optimizer=Adam(0.0002, 0.5), loss='binary_crossentropy') # Training the GAN def train_gan(epochs, batch_size): for epoch in range(epochs): # Train discriminator idx = np.random.randint(0, x_train.shape[0], batch_size) real_images = x_train[idx] noise = np.random.normal(0, 1, (batch_size, 100))
```

```python
fake_images = generator.predict(noise)
d_loss_real = discriminator.train_on_batch(real_images, np.ones((batch_size, 1)))
d_loss_fake = discriminator.train_on_batch(fake_images, np.zeros((batch_size, 1)))
d_loss = 0.5 * np.add(d_loss_real, d_loss_fake)
# Train generator
noise = np.random.normal(0, 1, (batch_size, 100))
valid_y = np.array([1] * batch_size)
g_loss = gan.train_on_batch(noise, valid_y)
print(f"Epoch {epoch+1}/{epochs} | D
```

Loss: {d_loss} | G Loss: {g_loss}")

```
train_gan(epochs=10000, batch_size=64)
```

Chapter 11: Style Transfer

Style transfer involves taking the style of one image and applying it to the content of another. Neural networks can extract stylistic features and blend them with the content features of different images, producing creative and visually appealing results.

Use Case: Artistic Style Transfer Artists and designers use style transfer to create new artworks by combining famous painting styles with their own photographs.

Example Code: Neural Style Transfer in Python

python

Copy code

```
import tensorflow as tf import numpy as np
import matplotlib.pyplot as plt from PIL
import Image from
tensorflow.keras.applications.vgg19 import
VGG19, preprocess_input from
tensorflow.keras.models import Model # Load
```

```python
and preprocess images
def load_and_process_img(path_to_img):
    img = Image.open(path_to_img)
    img = img.resize((400, 400))
    img = tf.keras.preprocessing.image.img_to_array(img)
    img = np.expand_dims(img, axis=0)
    img = preprocess_input(img)
    return img

content_image = load_and_process_img('path_to_content_image.jpg')
style_image = load_and_process_img('path_to_style_image.jpg')

# Load the VGG19 model
vgg =
```

```
VGG19(include_top=False, weights='imagenet')

content_layers = ['block5_conv2'] style_layers =
['block1_conv1', 'block2_conv1', 'block3_conv1',
'block4_conv1', 'block5_conv1'] output_layers =
[vgg.get_layer(name).output for name in
(style_layers + content_layers)] model =
Model([vgg.input], output_layers) # Define the
loss functions and optimizers def
compute_loss(model, loss_weights, init_image,
gram_style_features, content_features):
style_weight, content_weight = loss_weights
model_outputs = model(init_image)
```

```python
style_output_features = model_outputs[:len(style_layers)]
content_output_features = model_outputs[len(style_layers):] style_score =
0 content_score = 0 # Style loss
weight_per_style_layer = 1.0 /
float(len(style_layers)) for target_style,
comb_style in zip(gram_style_features,
style_output_features): style_score +=
weight_per_style_layer *
tf.reduce_mean(tf.square(target_style -
comb_style)) # Content loss
```

```python
weight_per_content_layer = 1.0 / float(len(content_layers))
    for target_content, comb_content in zip(content_features, content_output_features):
        content_score += weight_per_content_layer * tf.reduce_mean(tf.square(target_content - comb_content))
    style_score *= style_weight
    content_score *= content_weight
    loss = style_score + content_score
    return loss

# Optimization loop to minimize the loss and generate the stylized image
import tensorflow.contrib.eager as tfe
def
```

```python
run_style_transfer(content_path, style_path,
num_iterations=1000, content_weight=1e3,
style_weight=1e-2): model = get_model() for
layer in model.layers: layer.trainable = False
style_features, content_features =
get_feature_representations(model,
content_path, style_path) gram_style_features =
[gram_matrix(style_feature) for style_feature in
style_features] init_image =
load_and_process_img(content_path) init_image
= tf.Variable(init_image, dtype=tf.float32) opt =
tf.train.AdamOptimizer(learning_rate=5,
```

```python
beta1=0.99, epsilon=1e-1) iter_count = 1

best_loss, best_img = float('inf'), None

loss_weights = (style_weight, content_weight)

norm_means = np.array([103.939, 116.779,
123.68]) min_vals = -norm_means max_vals =
255 - norm_means for i in
range(num_iterations): with tf.GradientTape()
as tape: all_loss = compute_loss(model,
loss_weights, init_image, gram_style_features,
content_features) total_loss = all_loss[0] grads
= tape.gradient(total_loss, init_image)
opt.apply_gradients([[(grads, init_image)]])
```

```python
        clipped = tf.clip_by_value(init_image, min_vals,
max_vals)        init_image.assign(clipped)        if
total_loss < best_loss: best_loss = total_loss
best_img = init_image.numpy() print(f'Iteration:
{i} Loss: {total_loss.numpy()}') return best_img,
best_loss        best_img,        best_loss        =
run_style_transfer('path_to_content_image.jpg',
'path_to_style_image.jpg')

plt.imshow(best_img[0]) plt.show()
```

Chapter 12: Super-Resolution

Super-resolution refers to the process of enhancing the resolution of an image, making it sharper and more detailed. Generative models can be trained to upscale low-resolution images effectively.

Use Case: Medical Imaging In medical imaging, super-resolution can help enhance the clarity of MRI or CT scans, leading to more accurate diagnoses.

Example Scenario A healthcare provider uses a GAN-based model to improve the resolution of MRI scans, enabling doctors to better detect and analyze small anomalies that may not be visible in lower-resolution images.

Example Code: Super-Resolution with SRCNN in Python

python

Copy code

```python
import numpy as np
import cv2
from keras.models import Sequential
from keras.layers import Conv2D

# Load and preprocess a low-resolution image
image = cv2.imread('low_resolution_image.jpg')
image = cv2.cvtColor(image, cv2.COLOR_BGR2YCrCb)
y, cr, cb = cv2.split(image)
y = y.astype('float32') / 255.0

# Define the SRCNN model
srcnn = Sequential()
srcnn.add(Conv2D(64, (9, 9), activation='relu', input_shape=(None, None, 1), padding='same'))
srcnn.add(Conv2D(32, (1, 1), activation='relu', padding='same'))
```

```python
srcnn.add(Conv2D(1, (5, 5), activation='linear',
padding='same'))
srcnn.compile(optimizer='adam',
loss='mean_squared_error') # Train the model
(assuming you have training data) #
srcnn.fit(X_train, y_train, epochs=100,
batch_size=64) # Super-resolve the image
input_image = y.reshape(1, y.shape[0],
y.shape[1], 1) output_image =
srcnn.predict(input_image) output_image =
output_image.reshape(y.shape[0], y.shape[1])
output_image = (output_image *
255.0).astype('uint8') # Combine with Cr and
```

Cb channels and save the image result =

cv2.merge((output_image, cr, cb)) result =

cv2.cvtColor(result, cv2.COLOR_YCrCb2BGR)

cv2.imwrite('high_resolution_image.jpg', result)

Chapter 13: Ethics and Challenges in Generative AI

Ethical Considerations

Generative AI poses several ethical challenges, including the potential for misuse in creating fake content, deepfakes, and privacy concerns.

Example Scenario Deepfake technology can create highly realistic videos of people saying or doing things they never did. This can be used maliciously to spread misinformation or damage reputations.

Case Study: Deepfakes and Misinformation

In 2019, a deepfake video of a politician went viral, causing widespread confusion and debate. The video, created using GANs, showed the politician making controversial statements they never actually made, illustrating the potential for generative AI to be used in harmful ways.

Bias and Fairness

Generative models can perpetuate and even amplify biases present in training data. Ensuring fairness and reducing bias is critical in developing responsible AI systems.

Example Scenario A facial recognition system trained on a biased dataset may generate biased outputs, disproportionately affecting certain demographic groups.

Example Code: Detecting Bias in GAN Outputs

```python
import numpy as np
import matplotlib.pyplot as plt

# Assuming `generated_images` is a batch of images generated by a GAN
generated_images = np.random.rand(100, 64, 64, 3)

# Analyze the distribution of features (e.g., skin tones)
skin_tones = [np.mean(img) for img in generated_images]

# Plot the distribution
plt.hist(skin_tones, bins=50, color='blue', alpha=0.7)
plt.xlabel('Skin Tone Intensity')
plt.ylabel('Frequency')
```

```python
plt.title('Distribution of Skin Tones in Generated Images')
plt.show()

# Check for bias
threshold = 0.5
biased_samples = [tone for tone in skin_tones if tone < threshold]
bias_ratio = len(biased_samples) / len(skin_tones)
print(f"Bias Ratio: {bias_ratio:.2f}")
```

Security Concerns

Generative AI can be exploited for malicious purposes, such as generating realistic phishing emails or bypassing security systems.

Example Scenario Cybercriminals use generative models to create sophisticated phishing emails that are difficult to distinguish from legitimate ones, increasing the risk of successful cyber attacks.

Future Challenges

As generative AI continues to evolve, it will face several challenges, including improving model transparency, ensuring ethical use, and addressing regulatory concerns.

Example Scenario Regulatory bodies may need to develop new guidelines to govern the use of generative AI, ensuring that it is used responsibly and ethically.

Part IV: Practical Applications and Case Studies

Chapter 14: Generative AI in Art and Creativity

AI-generated Art

Generative models can create original artworks, blending various styles and techniques to produce novel and unique pieces.

Example Scenario Artists use GANs to generate new pieces of art by training on datasets of classical paintings. The result is a series of modern artworks that incorporate elements from different art movements.

Case Study: AI Art Auction In 2018, an AI-generated artwork created using GANs was sold at auction for $432,500, highlighting the growing interest and value of AI in the art world.

Music and Literature

AI can generate music and literary content, offering new tools for composers and writers to explore creative possibilities.

Example Scenario A composer uses an AI model trained on a dataset of classical music to generate new compositions, which they then refine and orchestrate for performance.

Example Code: Generating Music with RNNs

python

Copy code

```
from music21 import converter, instrument,
note, chord, stream import numpy as np from
keras.models import Sequential from
keras.layers import LSTM, Dense, Dropout
from keras.utils import np_utils # Load and
preprocess music data midi =
converter.parse('path_to_midi_file.mid') notes
= [] for element in midi.flat.notes: if
```

```python
        isinstance(element, note.Note):
            notes.append(str(element.pitch))
        elif isinstance(element, chord.Chord):
            notes.append('.'.join(str(n) for n in element.normalOrder))

# Prepare the data for training
sequence_length = 100
pitchnames = sorted(set(notes))
n_vocab = len(pitchnames)
note_to_int = dict((note, number) for number, note in enumerate(pitchnames))

network_input = []
network_output = []
for i in range(0, len(notes) - sequence_length, 1):
    seq_in = notes[i:i + sequence_length]
    seq_out =
```

```python
notes[i + sequence_length]
network_input.append([note_to_int[char] for char in seq_in])
network_output.append(note_to_int[seq_out])
n_patterns = len(network_input)
network_input = np.reshape(network_input, (n_patterns, sequence_length, 1))
network_input = network_input / float(n_vocab)
network_output = np_utils.to_categorical(network_output) # Define the RNN model model = Sequential()
model.add(LSTM(256,
```

```python
    input_shape=(network_input.shape[1],

    network_input.shape[2]),

    return_sequences=True))

model.add(Dropout(0.3))

model.add(LSTM(256,

    return_sequences=True))

model.add(Dropout(0.3))

model.add(LSTM(256))

model.add(Dense(128))

model.add(Dropout(0.3))

model.add(Dense(n_vocab,

    activation='softmax'))
```

```python
model.compile(loss='categorical_crossentropy',
optimizer='adam') # Train the model
model.fit(network_input, network_output,
epochs=200, batch_size=64) # Generate new
music start = np.random.randint(0,
len(network_input) - 1) pattern =
network_input[start] prediction_output = [] for
note_index in range(500): prediction_input =
np.reshape(pattern, (1, len(pattern), 1))
prediction_input = prediction_input /
float(n_vocab) prediction = model.predict(pred
```

Case Studies

Real-world Implementations

Generative AI has found diverse applications across industries, demonstrating its versatility and impact in solving real-world problems. Here are some examples of successful implementations:

Healthcare - Drug Discovery: Pharmaceutical companies utilize generative models to accelerate the drug discovery process. By generating novel molecular structures, these models help identify potential drug candidates faster and more efficiently than traditional methods.

Finance - Fraud Detection: Financial institutions employ generative models to detect fraudulent activities by generating realistic scenarios that expose vulnerabilities in existing systems. This aids in preventing financial crimes and protecting customer assets.

Success Stories

Generative AI has led to remarkable success stories, showcasing its transformative potential in various domains:

Entertainment - Movie Industry: In the movie industry, generative AI is used to create stunning visual effects, realistic backgrounds, and even virtual characters. This technology has revolutionized filmmaking, enabling filmmakers to bring their creative visions to life in ways previously unimaginable.

Education - Personalized Learning: Educational institutions leverage generative models to personalize learning experiences for students. By generating tailored educational materials and adaptive tutoring systems, these models enhance student engagement and learning outcomes.

Lessons Learned

Implementing generative AI comes with valuable lessons and insights:

Data Quality and Diversity: High-quality, diverse data is essential for training effective generative models. Organizations must invest in data collection and curation to ensure their models produce accurate and reliable outputs.

Ethical Considerations: Generative AI raises ethical concerns, such as bias and privacy. It is crucial to address these concerns proactively by implementing ethical guidelines and fairness checks in model development and deployment.

Part V: Tools and Frameworks

Deep Learning Frameworks

Deep learning frameworks provide the foundation for building and deploying generative models. Here are three popular frameworks:

TensorFlow: Developed by Google, TensorFlow is a versatile deep learning framework known for its flexibility and scalability. It offers a comprehensive ecosystem for building various machine learning models, including generative models like GANs and VAEs.

PyTorch: Developed by Facebook, PyTorch is a dynamic deep learning framework favored by researchers and practitioners for its intuitive interface and Pythonic syntax. It provides a seamless experience for prototyping and experimenting with generative models.

Keras: Keras is a high-level deep learning library that runs on top of TensorFlow and other backend engines. It offers a user-friendly API for building and training neural networks, making it accessible to beginners and experts alike.

These frameworks provide powerful tools and abstractions for implementing generative AI solutions, empowering developers to explore new possibilities and innovate in the field

Part IV: Practical Applications and Case Studies

Chapter 17: Case Studies

Real-world Implementations

Generative AI has been successfully implemented in various industries, demonstrating its versatility and potential. These real-world implementations showcase how businesses and organizations leverage generative models to innovate and solve complex problems.

Example Scenario: Healthcare - Drug Discovery Pharmaceutical companies are using generative models to accelerate drug discovery. By generating novel molecular structures, these models help identify potential drug candidates faster than traditional methods.

Case Study: Insilico Medicine Insilico Medicine uses GANs to generate new molecular structures for drug discovery. Their AI-driven approach has significantly reduced the time and cost involved in identifying promising compounds for further development.

Example Scenario: Automotive - Autonomous Vehicles Generative models play a crucial role in developing autonomous vehicles. They generate realistic driving scenarios for training and testing self-driving algorithms, improving the safety and reliability of autonomous systems.

Case Study: Waymo Waymo, a leader in autonomous driving, employs generative models to simulate diverse driving conditions. This helps train their AI systems to handle a wide range of scenarios, from common road conditions to rare and hazardous situations.

Success Stories

Success stories in generative AI highlight how organizations have achieved remarkable outcomes by integrating these technologies into their workflows. These stories demonstrate the transformative impact of generative AI across various domains.

Example Scenario: Entertainment - Movie Industry In the movie industry, generative AI is used to create special effects, generate realistic backgrounds, and even bring characters to life.

Case Study: Disney's CGI Innovations Disney uses generative models to enhance their CGI capabilities. For instance, they employed generative AI to create lifelike animal characters in "The Lion King" (2019), resulting in visually stunning and highly realistic animations.

Example Scenario: Finance - Fraud Detection Financial institutions utilize generative models to detect fraudulent activities by generating realistic scenarios that expose vulnerabilities in existing systems.

Case Study: JPMorgan Chase JPMorgan Chase implemented generative models to improve their fraud detection mechanisms. By generating synthetic transaction data, they trained their AI systems to identify and prevent fraudulent activities more effectively, enhancing overall security.

Lessons Learned

While generative AI offers immense potential, its implementation comes with challenges and learning opportunities. Understanding these lessons can help future adopters navigate the complexities of deploying generative models.

Lesson 1: Data Quality and Quantity High-quality, diverse data is crucial for training effective generative models. Organizations must invest in data collection and curation to ensure their models are well-trained and accurate.

Lesson 2: Model Interpretability

Understanding how generative models make decisions is essential for trust and transparency. Developing methods to interpret and explain model outputs can enhance user confidence and regulatory compliance.

Lesson 3: Ethical Considerations Ethical concerns, such as bias and misuse, must be addressed proactively. Establishing ethical guidelines and implementing fairness checks can mitigate potential risks associated with generative AI.

Lesson 4: Continuous Learning and Adaptation Generative models require continuous learning and adaptation to remain effective. Regular updates and retraining on new data ensure that models evolve and improve over time.

Part V: Tools and Frameworks

Chapter 18: Deep Learning Frameworks

TensorFlow

TensorFlow, developed by Google, is a widely-used deep learning framework that supports various machine learning tasks, including generative models. It offers a flexible and comprehensive ecosystem for building and deploying AI applications.

Key Features:

- Extensive library of pre-built models and algorithms.

- Support for distributed computing and scalable training.

- Tools for model visualization, debugging, and optimization.

Example Code: Simple GAN in TensorFlow

python

Copy code

```python
import tensorflow as tf from tensorflow.keras
import layers # Define the generator model def
build_generator(): model = tf.keras.Sequential([
layers.Dense(128,                      activation='relu',
input_dim=100),  layers.BatchNormalization(),
layers.Dense(256,                      activation='relu'),
layers.BatchNormalization(), layers.Dense(512,
activation='relu'), layers.BatchNormalization(),
layers.Dense(784, activation='tanh') ])  return
model # Define the discriminator model def
build_discriminator():              model          =
tf.keras.Sequential([              layers.Dense(512,
```

```python
                input_dim=784,                    activation='relu'),

    layers.Dense(256,                    activation='relu'),

    layers.Dense(1, activation='sigmoid') ]) return

model  #  Compile  the  models  generator  =

build_generator()        discriminator        =

build_discriminator()

discriminator.compile(optimizer='adam',

loss='binary_crossentropy')

discriminator.trainable = False  # Combine the

models   to   form   the   GAN   gan_input   =

tf.keras.Input(shape=(100,))  generated_image

=    generator(gan_input)    gan_output    =
```

```python
discriminator(generated_image) gan =
tf.keras.Model(gan_input, gan_output)
gan.compile(optimizer='adam',
loss='binary_crossentropy') # Train the GAN
def train_gan(epochs, batch_size): for epoch in
range(epochs): noise =
tf.random.normal([batch_size, 100])
generated_images = generator(noise)
real_images = tf.random.normal([batch_size,
784]) # Replace with real data labels_real =
tf.ones((batch_size, 1)) labels_fake =
tf.zeros((batch_size, 1)) d_loss_real =
```

```python
discriminator.train_on_batch(real_images,
labels_real)                    d_loss_fake         =
discriminator.train_on_batch(generated_images,
labels_fake) d_loss = 0.5 * tf.add(d_loss_real,
d_loss_fake)                    noise               =
tf.random.normal([batch_size,              100])
valid_labels = tf.ones((batch_size, 1)) g_loss =
gan.train_on_batch(noise,           valid_labels)
print(f"Epoch {epoch+1}/{epochs} | D Loss:
{d_loss}     |     G     Loss:     {g_loss}")
train_gan(epochs=10000, batch_size=64)
```

PyTorch

PyTorch, developed by Facebook, is another popular deep learning framework known for its dynamic computation graph and ease of use. It is widely adopted for research and development due to its flexibility and integration with Python.

Key Features:

- Dynamic computation graph for easy debugging and iterative development.

- Extensive library of pre-trained models and tools.

- Strong community support and comprehensive documentation.

Example Code: Simple GAN in PyTorch

python

Copy code

```python
import torch import torch.nn as nn import torch.optim as optim # Define the generator model class Generator(nn.Module): def _init_(self): super(Generator, self)._init_()
```

```python
        self.model = nn.Sequential( nn.Linear(100,
128), nn.ReLU(True), nn.Linear(128, 256),
nn.ReLU(True),      nn.Linear(256,      512),
nn.ReLU(True), nn.Linear(512, 784), nn.Tanh() )
    def forward(self, x): return self.model(x) #
Define the discriminator model class
Discriminator(nn.Module): def __init__(self):
super(Discriminator, self).__init__() self.model =
nn.Sequential(      nn.Linear(784,      512),
nn.ReLU(True),      nn.Linear(512,      256),
nn.ReLU(True), nn.Linear(256, 1), nn.Sigmoid() )
    def forward(self, x): return self.model(x) #
```

```python
# Instantiate models and optimizers
generator = Generator()
discriminator = Discriminator()

optimizer_G = optim.Adam(generator.parameters(), lr=0.0002)
optimizer_D = optim.Adam(discriminator.parameters(), lr=0.0002)
loss_function = nn.BCELoss()

# Training the GAN
def train_gan(epochs, batch_size):
    for epoch in range(epochs):
        # Train discriminator
        noise = torch.randn(batch_size, 100)
        fake_images = generator(noise)
        real_images =
```

```python
torch.randn(batch_size, 784) # Replace with
real data labels_real = torch.ones(batch_size, 1)
labels_fake = torch.zeros(batch_size, 1)
optimizer_D.zero_grad() output_real =
discriminator(real_images) loss_real =
loss_function(output_real, labels_real)
output_fake =
discriminator(fake_images.detach()) loss_fake
= loss_function(output_fake, labels_fake) loss_D
= (loss_real + loss_fake) / 2 loss_D.backward()
optimizer_D.step() # Train generator
optimizer_G.zero_grad() output =
```

```
discriminator(fake_images)        loss_G        =
loss_function(output,                labels_real)
loss_G.backward()          optimizer_G.step()
print(f"Epoch  {epoch+1}/{epochs}  |  D  Loss:
{loss_D.item()}  |  G  Loss:  {loss_G.item()}")
train_gan(epochs=10000, batch_size=64)
```

Keras

Keras is an open-source neural network library written in Python. It is designed to enable fast experimentation with deep neural networks, being both user-friendly and modular. Keras is now part of the TensorFlow ecosystem, providing a high-level interface for TensorFlow.

Key Features:

- Simplified API for building and training models.

- Integration with TensorFlow for backend operations.

- Extensive community support and documentation.

Example Code: Simple GAN in Keras

python

Copy code

```python
from keras.models import Sequential from
keras.layers import Dense, LeakyReLU from
keras.optimizers import Adam import numpy
as np # Define the generator model def
build_generator(): model = Sequential()
model.add(Dense(256, input_dim=100))
model.add(LeakyReLU(alpha=0.2))
model.add(Dense(512))
model.add(LeakyReLU(alpha=0.2))
model.add(Dense(1024))
model.add(LeakyReLU(alpha=0.2))
```

```python
    model.add(Dense(784, activation='tanh'))
    return model # Define the discriminator model
def build_discriminator(): model = Sequential()
    model.add(Dense(1024, input_dim=784))
    model.add(LeakyReLU(alpha=0.2))
    model.add(Dense(512))
    model.add(LeakyReLU(alpha=0.2))
    model.add(Dense(256))
    model.add(LeakyReLU(alpha=0.2))
    model.add(Dense(1, activation='sigmoid'))
    return model # Compile the models generator
= build_generator() discriminator =
```

```
build_discriminator()

discriminator.compile(optimizer=Adam(),

loss='binary_crossentropy')

discriminator.trainable = False # Combine the

models to form the GAN gan_input =

keras.Input(shape=(100,)) generated_image =

generator(gan_input)       gan_output       =

discriminator(generated_image)       gan       =

keras.Model(gan_input,            gan_output)

gan.compile(optimizer=Adam(),

loss='binary_crossentropy') # Train the GAN

def train_gan(epochs, batch_size): for epoch in
```

```
range(epochs): noise = np.random.normal(0, 1,
(batch_size, 100)) generated_images =
generator.predict(noise) real_images =
np.random.normal(0, 1, (batch_size, 784)) #
Replace with real data labels_real =
np.ones((batch_size, 1)) labels_fake =
np.zeros((batch_size, 1)) d_loss_real =
discriminator.train_on_batch(real_images,
labels_real) d_loss_fake =
discriminator.train_on_batch(generated_images,
labels_fake) d_loss = 0.5 * np.add(d_loss_real,
d_loss_fake) noise = np.random.normal(0, 1,
```

```python
(batch_size, 100)) valid_labels =
np.ones((batch_size, 1)) g_loss =
gan.train_on_batch(noise, valid_labels)

print(f"Epoch {epoch+1}/{epochs} | D Loss:
{d_loss} | G Loss: {g_loss}")

train_gan(epochs=10000, batch_size=64)
```

Chapter 19: Generative AI Tools and Libraries

OpenAI GPT

OpenAI's Generative Pre-trained Transformer (GPT) is a state-of-the-art language model that can generate human-like text. It has been widely adopted for tasks such as text completion, translation, and creative writing.

Key Features:

- Large-scale language model with billions of parameters.

- Ability to generate coherent and contextually relevant text.

- Versatility in various natural language processing tasks.

Example Scenario: Content Creation A company uses GPT to generate marketing copy for their products, saving time and resources while maintaining high-quality content.

Example Code: Using GPT for Text Generation

python

Copy code

```
import openai openai.api_key =
'your_api_key_here' response =
openai.Completion.create( model="text-
davinci-003", prompt="Write a promotional
email for a new product launch.",
max_tokens=200 )
print(response.choices[0].text.strip())
```

StyleGAN

StyleGAN, developed by NVIDIA, is a
generative adversarial network designed to

generate high-quality images. It allows for fine-grained control over the style and features of the generated images.

Key Features:

- High-quality image generation with fine control over style.

- Versatile in generating various types of images, from portraits to landscapes.

- Advanced architecture for improved image synthesis.

Example Scenario: Custom Avatar Creation

A gaming company uses StyleGAN to generate custom avatars for players, providing a unique and personalized gaming experience.

Example Code: Using StyleGAN for Image Generation

python

Copy code

```
import numpy as np import matplotlib.pyplot as plt import dnnlib import dnnlib.tflib as tflib import pretrained_networks # Load pre-
```

```
trained StyleGAN model network_pkl =
'gdrive:networks/stylegan2-ffhq-config-f.pkl'
_G, _D, Gs =
pretrained_networks.load_networks(network_p
kl) # Generate a random image rnd =
np.random.RandomState(5) latents =
rnd.randn(1, Gs.input_shape[1]) images =
Gs.run(latents, None) # Display the image
plt.imshow(images[0]) plt.show()
```

DeepArt

DeepArt is a tool that uses neural networks to apply artistic styles to images. It enables users to transform their photos into artworks inspired by famous artists and art movements.

Key Features:

- Application of artistic styles to images using deep learning.

- Customization of style intensity and blending.

- User-friendly interface for easy transformation of images.

Example Scenario: Photo to Artwork Transformation An artist uses DeepArt to transform their photographs into artworks inspired by Van Gogh, creating a unique blend of photography and painting.

Example Code: Using DeepArt for Style Transfer

python

Copy code

```
import requests # API endpoint and key url =
'https://api.deepart.io/api/artwork' api_key =
'your_api_key_here' # Upload images files = {
'image': open('path_to_image.jpg', 'rb'), 'style':
```

```
open('path_to_style_image.jpg', 'rb') } data =
{'api_key':      api_key}      response      =
requests.post(url,    files=files,    data=data)
print(response.json())
```

Chapter 20: Building and Deploying Generative Models

Model Training and Evaluation

Training generative models involves optimizing their parameters to generate realistic and high-quality outputs. Evaluation metrics such as Inception Score and Frechet

Inception Distance help assess the performance of these models.

Example Scenario: Training a GAN A researcher trains a GAN on a dataset of landscape images to generate new, photorealistic landscapes.

Example Code: Training and Evaluating a GAN

python

Copy code

Training and evaluation code (see previous GAN examples for detailed implementation)

Deployment Strategies

Deploying generative models involves making them accessible to users and ensuring they perform well in real-world conditions. Strategies include using cloud services, setting up APIs, and optimizing models for different platforms.

Example Scenario: Deploying a Text Generation Model A company deploys a GPT-based chatbot on their website to handle customer queries, providing instant and accurate responses.

Example Code: Deploying a Model as a Web Service

python

Copy code

```
from flask import Flask, request, jsonify import
openai app = Flask(__name__) openai.api_key =
'your_api_key_here' @app.route('/generate',
methods=['POST']) def generate(): data =
request.get_json() prompt = data['prompt']
response = openai.Completion.create(
```

```
model="text-davinci-003",      prompt=prompt,
max_tokens=200   )   return   jsonify({'text':
response.choices[0].text.strip()})   if   _name_
== '_main_': app.run()
```

Scaling and Optimization

Scaling generative models to handle large volumes of requests requires efficient use of resources and optimization techniques. This includes model quantization, distributed computing, and using specialized hardware like GPUs and TPUs.

Example Scenario: Scaling an Image Generation Service A social media platform scales their image generation service to handle millions of daily requests by optimizing their models and infrastructure.

Example Code: Optimizing Model Performance

python

Copy code

```
import tensorflow as tf # Model quantization example converter =
```

```
tf.lite.TFLiteConverter.from_keras_model(gener
ator)          converter.optimizations          =
[tf.lite.Optimize.DEFAULT]     tflite_model     =
converter.convert()  #  Save  the  quantized
model with open('quantized_model.tflite', 'wb')
as f: f.write(tflite_model)
```

Part VI: Future Directions

Chapter 21: The Future of Generative AI and Deep Learning

Emerging Trends

Generative AI and deep learning continue to evolve, with emerging trends such as multimodal models, self-supervised learning, and generative pre-trained transformers shaping the future of AI research and applications.

Example Scenario: Multimodal Models

Multimodal models that combine text, image, and audio data are being developed to create more comprehensive AI systems that can understand and generate content across different modalities.

Research Directions

Future research in generative AI aims to address challenges like improving model interpretability, reducing bias, and enhancing the efficiency and scalability of generative models.

Example Scenario: Reducing Bias in AI

Researchers are developing techniques to reduce bias in generative models, ensuring fair and unbiased outputs across different demographic groups.

Impact on Society

Generative AI has the potential to transform various aspects of society, from enhancing creative industries to revolutionizing healthcare and education. However, it also raises ethical and societal concerns that need to be addressed.

Example Scenario: AI in Education

Generative AI is used to create personalized learning materials and tutoring systems, improving educational outcomes and accessibility.

Conclusion

Recap of Key Concepts

This guide covered the fundamentals of generative AI, including key techniques like GANs and VAEs, practical applications across various industries, and the tools and frameworks used to build and deploy generative models. We also explored ethical considerations, real-world case studies, and future directions in the field.

Final Thoughts

Generative AI holds immense potential to innovate and transform industries, but it must be developed and deployed responsibly. As the technology continues to advance, addressing ethical challenges and ensuring fair and unbiased outcomes will be crucial to harnessing its full potential for the benefit of society.

www.ingramcontent.com/pod-product-compliance
Lightning Source LLC
LaVergne TN
LVHW051341050326
832903LV00031B/3677